BLACK—WHITE—RED

MYNONA

A.K.A. SALOMO FRIEDLAENDER

BLACK–WHITE–RED

Grotesques

WITH TWO DRAWINGS BY LUDWIG MEIDNER

TRANSLATED BY W. C. BAMBERGER

WAKEFIELD PRESS

CAMBRIDGE, MASSACHUSETTS

This translation © 2022 WAKEFIELD PRESS

Wakefield Press, P.O. Box 425645, Cambridge, MA 02142

Originally published as *Schwarz–Weiss–Rot: Grotesken von Mynona* (Mit Zwei Zeichnungen von L. Meidner) by Kurt Wolff Verlag in 1916.

Cover illustration and frontispiece by Ludwig Meidner © Ludwig Meidner-Archiv, Jüdisches Museum der Stadt Frankfurt am Main.

This book was set in Garamond Premier Pro and Helvetica Neue Pro by Wakefield Press. Printed and bound by McNaughton & Gunn, Inc., in the United States of America.

ISBN: 978-1-939663-84-9

Available through D.A.P./Distributed Art Publishers
75 Broad Street, Suite 630
New York, New York 10004
Tel: (212) 627-1999
Fax: (212) 627-9484

10 9 8 7 6 5 4 3 2 1

CONTENTS

TRANSLATOR'S INTRODUCTION

Salomo Friedlaender was born 4 May 1871 in Gollantsch, Posen, now part of Poland but then part of Germany. He studied medicine, but soon turned his attention to philosophy, literature, and art. He wrote his dissertation on Schopenhauer and Kant in 1899. He went on to write a number of philosophical works and published these under his original name, reserving Mynona for his literary output. His greatest renown came from his grotesques.

Schwarz–Weiss–Rot, the collection translated here, was first published in December 1916. Mynona, the author's name that appeared on the title page, is the German word for "anonymous" reversed. While many readers might not have known the author's true name, most would have understood this was a pseudonym.[1] This book was a follow-up to Friedlaender's first collection of "grotesques," *Rosa die schöne Gutzmannsfrau und andere Grotesken* (Rosa the beautiful policeman's wife and other grotesques), which had been published three years earlier and had attracted a great deal of positive attention for the author. "Grotesques" was the name Friedlaender/Mynona (hereafter F/M) gave to his short fictions that combined elements of the Gothic, horror and ghost stories, fairy tales, sexual fetishism, philosophy and slapstick comedy, antibourgeois sentiments and social commentary, romantic rapture, and more.

Ellen Otten, editor of a 1965 edition of selected writings by F/M (which was also titled *Rosa die schöne Gutzmannsfrau und andere Grotesken*), addressed the sensation the appearance of the first of these created:

> Today the grotesque has long been a familiar stylistic device, a legitimate mode of expression in modern theater, literature and cabaret. When—more than fifty years ago—the first grotesques by Mynona appeared, they seemed sensational, offensive, alienating and encouraging, invigorating, and pointing to new directions for the avant-garde of that time.[2]

Otten goes on to quote Albert Soergel, editor of *Dichtung und Dichter der Zeit*, an encyclopedic study of German literature from circa 1880 to the 1920s:

> The expressionistic grotesque grows out of its creator's conviction of being a universal being, grows out of an infinitely heightened self-confidence of thought, out of the conviction of freedom of the creative mind. It is no coincidence that the most characteristic creator of grotesque stories is a philosopher who wrote about Kant, Schopenhauer, Nietzsche, Robert Mayer, but also about Jean Paul as a thinker and about George Grosz: Salomo Friedlaender [who] uses a

poetic form such as the grotesque as a willing vessel that can be filled with products of thought that can hardly be expressed in today's forms of thought.[3]

Otten qualifies Soergel's comment:

Mynona's "products of thought" cast in the form of the grotesque are by no means derived from his philosophical knowledge, nor so to speak popularized intellectual science; rather they could be described as "applied philosophy," as wisdom that appears in the guise of a mocker. Unlimited imagination, especially in what is now called science fiction, where he meets his friend Paul Scheerbart, is perhaps the most striking characteristic of his grotesques. In addition, there is a sharp criticism of the times, which shows the keen ear and the vigilance of this critical spirit.[4]

The first work here, "Black–White–Red, or Germany's Victory over England under the Standard of Goethe's Colors," is less a story than a mock-nationalist manifesto. (Black, white, and red were the colors of the flag of the German empire from 1871 to 1919.) The scientifically literate and politically aggressive narrator treats the color theories of Goethe and Newton as standard bearers of national pride.

In an essay on Goethe's influence on German modernism, Andreas Kramer sums up the technique of this brief grotesque by pointing out how

Friedlaender uses the rhetoric and hollow formulae of German war propaganda in order to satirize them. [. . .]

Mynona's story is a tongue-in-cheek satire on prevailing nationalist attitudes and on the misappropriation of Goethe's thinking for political purposes.[5]

So effective was F/M at imitating the rhetorical style of the rabid nationalist that not everyone understood that the story was a satire. In his introduction to the first volume of F/M's collected grotesques, Detlef Thiel notes that although "Black–White–Red" was first published in the *Berliner Börsen-Courier* in October 1914, it was quoted a decade later by the German nationalist *National-post*. Some one hundred lines were reprinted, its sentiments taken at face value, as if F/M were a "literary champion of the flag."[6]

"Black–White–Red" was not the first time F/M mocked nationalism and militarism in his grotesques. In the first collection *Rosa die schöne Gutzmannsfrau*, F/M had included "Unter Kanonenkoenigen" (Among cannon kings).[7] Here the redheaded son of a munitions manufacturer proposes improving the appearance of his father's cannons by painting them white, "the color of innocence." Neither suitable metal nor paint is available, so the son sets off to invent something appropriate. In a farcical touch, the son studies almost everything except metallurgy: he studies "mysticism, heraldry, genealogy, entomology, gynecology, economics, Assyriology, philately, philanthropy, Kabbalah, theosophy, and social studies." Using this knowledge, he invents a new kind of steel—"from which all darkness has been removed by a certain process," which turns it silver-white. But when the first thirty-two white cannons are fired, they glow red and remain so; the inventor's father falls dead. In answer to the idea that war should be as harmless to look at as peace, the grotesque's moral is "Mars will always show its red color." In a further color-coded ironic touch, the son's red hair soon turns gray, then white.

Kramer notes that F/M "exhibited an unwavering fascination with Goethe throughout his life." He wrote essays about Goethe's life, a poem about his color theory, and always carried a prism in his pocket so he could demonstrate Goethe's theory when any doubts would arise.[8] F/M considered Goethe's theory of colors to be his greatest discovery:

> The struggle of Goethe versus Newton is the struggle of a deeper Monism, one that still knows how to reckon with opposing magnitudes, versus a shallower, more comfortable one. . . . The light- or color-opposition is as fundamental as the magnetic, the electrical, the sexual, the acoustic—as difference itself.[9]

Kramer points out Goethe's influence on F/M's philosophy, how he "channeled Goethe's color theory into a much wider context, developing a philosophy that he based on the principle of polarity or difference."[10] This refers to F/M's theory of "creative indifference," a philosophical position urging the individual to find the exact point of equilibrium between what are generally considered to be opposites. From such points, F/M held, we can engage with the world in truly creative ways. F/M's description of the fundamental importance of "light- or color-opposition" illustrates what he took from his reading of Goethe's theory.

Further evidence of F/M's fascination with Goethe and his theories can be found in the longest story in this collection, comprising nearly half of its total length, "Goethe Speaks into the Phonograph: A Love Story." Anna Pomke, a young follower of the Goethe cult, expresses her wish that the phonograph had been invented during Goethe's lifetime so that she could hear his voice. She addresses this remark to Professor Abnossah Pschorr, a famous engineer. Pschorr is secretly smitten with Anna and sets about trying to make her wish come true. This he is able to do, by way of a convoluted series of strategies, subterfuges, and some unique inventions.

F/M read and wrote about philosophers, and some philosophers have read and written about his work in return. "Goethe Speaks into the Phonograph" first appeared in English in a translation of media theorist Friedrich Kittler's *Gramophone, Film, Typewriter*.[11] Kittler's analysis of the nine-page story runs slightly longer. Only moderately tongue-in-cheek, Kittler analyzes what would have been necessary for Pschorr's recovery invention to actually work: Pschorr's optimism "depends upon the necessary but suppressed premise that infinite amplification could be applied," which only became remotely possible with advances in electronics a short decade before F/M wrote the grotesque. "Short stories of 1916 require the most up to date technologies," Kittler says. He adds, "From imagination to data processing, from the arts to the particulars of information technology and physiology—that is the historic shift of 1900 which Abnossah Pschorr must comprehend as well."[12] F/M clearly kept up with contemporary scientific achievements. For Kittler, Pschorr's undertaking is a contest between technology's new media and classical–Romantic poetics, a competition ultimately won by media.

In "The Magic Egg" the narrator is wandering through a vast desert.[13] In the middle of the desert rises a magnificent egg. The narrator first thinks it is a mirage but taps on it and finds it to be real. Buttons on the egg cause it to sink into the sand and to rise again. Upon further exploration a yolk is revealed. In a sly echo of Shelley's "Ozymandias," the narrator finds an inscription written on the yolk that proclaims the egg's magnificence: "Wanderer in the desert [. . .] know this: / That this egg alone can / transform the desert into Eden." The narrator enters the egg and explores its vast interior. In the end the egg expels him back into the desert sand. However, a mummy follows him out and explains how he can use the egg to redeem the world, to restore its "fertile power," and in the process experience the feeling of becoming divine. The mummy then expectantly reenters the egg, confident the narrator will act. The narrator briefly stands and wonders whether he should follow the mummy's instructions and accept responsibility for the world's redemption. Then, tucking his coattails under his arms, he flees the scene, "faster than any camel could."

In her essay "Messianic Endgames in German–Jewish Literature," Vivian Liska offers a reading of "The Magic Egg." She summarizes F/M's philosophy of "creative indifference" as addressing "the possibility of reconciling polarities and undoing contrasts" in redemptive action, and in this light sees the egg, which is entered by way of a joint that bisects it—that is, divides it into halves—as being "the perfect site for the annunciation of the possibility to save the universe."[14] This certainly is F/M's intent, and the egg's descent to the center of the Earth that would be triggered should the narrator follow the mummy's instructions reinforces this. But in the end, "The Magic Egg" is a story of a missed opportunity, of human doubt and perpetual indecision, of our inability to take action, of an individual's refusal to redeem the world even by doing something as simple as pushing a button.

"Broken Off" is a fragmentary, mock-serial account of a group of individuals (all suicides) rising from their graves and driving off in their casket cars to speak with their loved ones. The narrator finds his wife, who gently teases him for his vanity, for the theatrical arrangement of his shroud, even as tears run down her face. Following an interlude of romantic mathematics, they part. The dead drivers convert their casket cars into casket airships and fly heavenward. The conclusion of the tale offers some sober, even troubling, advice from those beyond the grave. "Tissue! Tissue!" comically portrays the difficulties involved in trying to do good deeds, to be generous and helpful in a world where cynical people, social conventions, and the law are all unequipped to cope with such unexpected behavior.

"Vertical Industry" is a combination instruction manual and sales brochure. It describes the creation, in a balloon hangar, of a kind of virtual reality experience: that of flying beyond Earth and through the solar system utilizing simple (early twentieth-century) mechanics. And at the end of this upbeat, enthusiastic exposition, the narrator, in a brief aside, leaves readers doubting the reality of the world itself.

Thus, at one pole F/M makes us doubt the existence of our world, while at the opposite pole he presents us with fascinating alternate worlds of his own invention. It is in the space between these poles that we read F/M.

NOTES

1. The title story is one of the handful of early grotesques credited to "Dr. S. Friedlaender" when it was first published in October 1914.

2. Ellen Otten, introduction to *Rosa die Schöne Schutzmannsfrau und Andere Grotesken*, ed. Ellen Otten (Zürich: Verlag der Arche, 1965), 237–244. This quote from 237. All translations from this and other sources cited are my own, unless otherwise noted.

3. Ibid., 238–239.

4. Ibid., 239.

5. Andreas Kramer, "Goethe and the Cultural Project of German Modernism: Steiner, Kandinsky, Friedlaender, Schwitters and Benjamin," *Publications of the English Goethe Society* 71, no. 1 (2001): 18–36, 31, https://doi.org/10.1080/09593683.2001.11716322.

6. Detlef Thiel, "Einleitung [Introduction]," in *Grotesken 1* (GS 7), ed. Detlef Thiel and Hartmut Geerken (Herrsching: waitawhile, 2008), 64. In part, this quotes cabaret artist Erich Weinert.

7. *Grotesken 1*, 205–207.

8. Kramer, "Goethe and the Cultural Project," 11.

9. Salomo Friedlaender, "Das Prisma und Goethes Farbenlehre" [The prism and Goethe's theory of colors], quoted in Kramer, "Goethe and the Cultural Project," 11.

10. Kramer, "Goethe and the Cultural Project," 11.

11. Friedrich A. Kittler, *Gramophone, Film, Typewriter*, trans. Geoffrey Winthrop-Young and Michael Wutz (Stanford: Stanford University Press, 1999). The story appears on 59–68.

12. Kittler, *Gramophone, Film, Typewriter*, 72–73.

13. "The Magic Egg" was previously translated in *Tales of the German Imagination from the Brothers Grimm to Ingeborg Bachmann*, trans. and ed. Peter Wortsman (London: Penguin Classics, 2013).

14. Vivian Liska, "Messianic Endgames in German–Jewish Literature," in *Europa! Europa? The Avant-Garde, Modernism and the Fate of a Continent*, ed. Sascha Bru, Jan Baetens, et al. (Berlin: De Gruyter, 2009), 351, 353.

BLACK–WHITE–RED

Grotesques

BLACK—WHITE—RED

or Germany's Victory over England under the Standard of Goethe's Colors

It is ominous in the highest degree that Germany quite literally flies Goethe's colors. To be specific, in addition to the extremes of all colors, white and black, there is red, which Goethe believed to be the color of all colors. And ominous in that Goethe, with his conception of colors, has for more than a century struggled in vain against England—namely, against the light-obscuring color doctrine of Isaac Newton, who, in a way that offends any fidelity of the German Goethe's eyes, alleges unbelievably false colors.

German science would have long since struck down the color-blind Englishman had he not isolated himself on the island of mathematics behind seemingly insurmountable barricades, and from there tyrannically brutalized the world of all colors for over two hundred years now. The Englishman teaches how to measure and to calculate; Goethe teaches how to see! And you should learn to see before you count and measure what you see. It is quite characteristic of the Englishman that he miscalculates because he is too hasty with his arithmetic—and, also, that for centuries the apparent precision of his calculations should conceal his highly erroneous approach. Let us hope that Goethe will prevail in Germany, in such a way that Germany's schoolchildren very soon will learn to laugh over the English colors that supposedly make up light, while for every German—i.e., good Goetheans, i.e., those with healthy eyes—they are clearly made of dark and light, of black and white, and in red have the dearest child of these parents:

> There are six siblings,
> Descendants of a wondrous twosome[1]

So said Schiller even before Goethe. This English prince of the mind, Newton, was a great mathematical master. But he is done for when Germany learns to see black and white in the Prussian manner and through Goethe's eyes: red will be calculated even more divine once it comes to see that this joyfully blushing gray between black and white stems as little from light alone as does the sober Prussian one, which is unmistakably a mixture of black and white. Don't be deceived by perfect English arithmetic, which is based on lies and deceit and the deception of the eye and lead your colors instead to the victory of German thoroughness under the Field Marshal of colors, Goethe, the über-Hindenburg of all color theory!

It's only because Goethe has also pointedly gone into the black that white has become capable of releasing color. The half-sighted Englishman developed them from white alone, for convenience's sake and also to be able to simplify calculations, but Goethe calculated too honestly for that, too deeply, and used the darkness, the black, as well. Does this not symbolically reflect our political conflict with a people who outwardly profess to shine as the most enlightened of lights, while inwardly concealing the color-barred treachery of total darkness, while the truly enlightened German Goethe freely and openly acknowledges black as well as white, and lets the iris of peace in between flare in color, which conducts its most solemn marriage in crimson?

To fail to appreciate that there is a real, true black, to act as if there were nothing but light, while concealing even the blackish indigo (!) within this seemingly pure light and, when you wish, to let it, in a calculated manner, burst forth—is that not English? And is it not quintessentially German and Goethean that Meister Schwarz—"Master Black"—invented black powder, and, further, that the color gray cannot be obtained from white alone—rather, only from the mixing of black and white, whose nearest offspring is red?[2]—If Germany wants to reconcile and unite the whole world, England wants to divide it, so that it might rule everywhere. Just so, Newton prefers to separate light within itself instead of marrying it with the lightless darkness that's not just grayish, but full of color:

Divide and rule!
A sound motto.
Unite and lead,
A better one.
—Goethe

England is all played out when it comes to color theory as well. German color theorists! At last, you are beginning to see that England is cheating you out of half the truth about color using cunning arithmetic, and that only Goethe gives you all of it. And Goethe, who laughs last, will also help you become a better mathematician, because he, like Kant, has the courage to openly and uncompromisingly take into account the negative magnitude, with the unvarnished minus and black of darkness, like Dr. Luther with the devil. This English light is only a different darkness, and Germany can learn from Goethe, as here:

Light and shadow
Coupled in true clarity

Black–white–red:—mother, father, child. All colors come together in this red, it is the fusion of orange, that is, heightened yellow, with violet, heightened blue, while blue and yellow mix into green, hope-rich root of the crown red. What a "miracle of meaning by chance" that the colors of Germany's flag constitute the true emblem of Goethean teaching![3] Goethe presented the opposition that needs to be reconciled, and he reconciles it nuptially in bright red. The cunning Englishman conceals the opposition, wraps it in innocent white, and seeks to subjugate it with a made-up, peace-loving, sterile unity that can hatch only warlike misbegotten monsters. Under the standard of Goethe, black–white–red, Germany shall also triumph scientifically! The murky gray of fate between light and darkness tears open, and the couple, miserably tortured by the Englishman, glow in the joyful red of their more intimate union:

> Now the world laughs,
> The gray curtain torn,
> The nuptials have come
> For light and darkness.[4]

GOETHE SPEAKS INTO THE PHONOGRAPH
A Love Story

"It's a shame," said Anna Pomke, a timid girl, suitably out-fitted with middle-class virtues, "that the phonograph hadn't already been invented in 1800!"

"Why?" asked Professor Abnossah Pschorr. "It is a shame, dear Pomke, that Eve didn't bring it as part of her dowry for that first savage marriage. Many things are a shame, dear Pomke."

"Oh, Professor, it would have been such a pleasure to have heard Goethe's voice! He is said to have had such a beautiful organ, and what he expressed with it was so rich. Oh, if only he had been able to speak into a phonograph! Oh! Oh!"

Pomke had left long before, but Abnossah, who had a fondness for her chirping chubbiness, could still hear her moans. Professor Pschorr, the inventor of the tactilestylus, sank into his habitual state of ingenious reflection. Should it not now be possible to posthumously trick this Goethe (Abnossah was absurdly jealous) out of the sound of his voice? When Goethe spoke, his voice always produced such regular vibrations, somewhat like the soft voice of your wife, dear reader. These vibrations encounter obstacles and are reflected, creating a back and forth which over time becomes weaker but can never actually come to an end. Therefore, those pulsing vibrations generated by Goethe's voice still remain, and you only need a suitable receiver to pick them up and a microphone to amplify the effects of their sound, which have since weakened, and Goethe's voice could again be made loud enough to be heard even today. The problem was the construction of the receiver. How could it be adjusted to the particular vibrations of Goethe's voice without the living Goethe speaking into it? An incredible story! To do this, Abnossah determined, the structure of Goethe's throat would have to be carefully studied. He looked at images and busts of Goethe, but these gave him only very vague impressions. He had nearly given up when he suddenly remembered that Goethe himself, if only in the form of his corpse, still existed. He immediately petitioned the Weimar authorities to be allowed to inspect Goethe's corpse for a short time, for the purpose of taking certain measurements. This petition, however, was turned down. What now?

Abnossah Pschorr, equipped with a small case full of the finest measuring and burglary tools, went to dear old Weimar. Incidentally, there in the first-class waiting room sat the locally renowned sister of a world-renowned brother, engaged in pleasant conversation with an elderly Highness from Rudolstadt. Abnossah only heard her say, "Our Fritz always had a military air about him, and yet he was gentle; he was gentle in the most Christian manner with others—how pleased he would have been with this war! And with that marvelous, even holy book by Max Scheler!"[5]

Abnossah was floored in horror. He pulled himself upright again only with difficulty and found lodgings in The Elephant. In his room he carefully examined his instruments. Then he moved a chair in front of the mirror and tried on nothing other than an astonishing portrait-like mask of dear old Goethe. He tied it on, covering his face, and spoke through it:

"You know that I am certainly a genius,

"Indeed, I may be Goethe himself!

"Make way, you devil! Or I will call for Schiller and Karl August, my prince, to help—you fool, you impostor!"

He rehearsed this speech, speaking in a sonorous, deep voice.

Late that night he set out for the princely tomb. Modern burglars, all of whom I hope number among my readers, will smile at those other readers who believe that a break-in at the well-guarded Weimar princely tomb is an impossibility. But you must remember that a Professor Pschorr, as a burglar, is immensely far ahead of even the most skillful of professional burglars! Pschorr is not only a skillful engineer; he is also a psycho-physiologist, a hypnotist, psychiatrist, psychoanalyst. Truly, it is a shame that there are so few educated criminals. If all criminals were successful, they would then finally be included in the nature of things and be as little subject to punishment as are natural phenomena. Who takes to task the lightning that melts Mr. Meier's fireproof safe? Burglars like Pschorr are superior to lightning because no diverter is proof against them.

Pschorr was able to horrify and, by means of hypnosis, effectively paralyze those guarding the gate, all in a single moment. Imagine it is midnight and you are guarding the royal tomb. Suddenly before you stands the elderly Goethe, who renders you immobile, so nothing of you lives other than just your head. Pschorr transformed the entire group of guards into such heads on dead-seeming torsos. Before the spasm relaxed, he had two hours, easily, and he made the most of them. He went into the tomb, flicked on a flashlight, and soon found Goethe's coffin. After a little effort he was on intimate terms with the corpse. Piety is good for people who have no other worries. That Pschorr handled Goethe's corpse expediently should not be held against him; he also took some wax impressions. In the time remaining he took pains to ensure that everything was restored to its proper order. Generally speaking, educated amateur criminals are truly more radical than professionals, but it is this radicalism, the precision of execution, that gives their crimes the aesthetic charm of mathematics and of a problem completely solved, with no remainder.

When Pschorr came out again into the open, he added still more elegance to this precision in that he intentionally freed a sentry from his paralysis and took him to task, just as he had rehearsed. He then immediately tore the mask from his face and, at a leisurely tempo, went back to The Elephant. He was pleased; he had what he'd come for. Early the next morning he returned home.

Now began a period of great activity. As you know, you can use a skeleton to construct a fully fleshed body. Pschorr, at any rate, was able to do so. There were no more insuperable difficulties in the way of exactly reproducing Goethe's airway as far as his vocal cords and lungs went. The timbre and strength of the sounds that these organs would produce was easy to determine—one only had to allow the stream of air that corresponded to Goethe's measured lung capacity to pass through. It was not long before Goethe spoke, as he must have spoken during his lifetime.

However, as it was a matter of reproducing not only his voice but also the words he had spoken in this voice a hundred years earlier, it was necessary to install Goethe's dummy in a room in which such words had often rung out.

Abnossah invited Pomke. She came and laughed at him in delight.

"Would you like to hear him speak?"

"Who?" Anna Pomke asked.

"Your Goethe."

"Mine? Come now, Professor!"

"Oh, yes!"

Abnossah wound up the phonograph and they heard:

"Friends, flee the dark chamber . . ." etc.

Pomke was strangely unsettled.

"Yes," she said hastily, "that is exactly how I imagined his organ—oh, it's so enchanting!"

"Of course," Pschorr cried. "But I do not wish to deceive you, my dear. Yes, it is Goethe, his voice, his words. However, not the actual replay of the actual words spoken by him. What you just heard was the replay of a possibility, not a reality. However, it is my intent to scrupulously fulfill your wish, and therefore I propose to you a joint journey to Weimar."

The locally known sister of the world-renowned brother once again sat in the waiting room of the Weimar railway station and whispered to an elderly lady: "There remains one final work written by my late brother that will only be brought out in the year 2000. The world is not yet ready for it. My brother had his ancestors' pious reverence in his blood. The world, however, is frivolous and would make no distinction between a satyr and this saint. The little people in Italy saw the saint in him."

Pomke would have fallen over if Pschorr had not caught her. This made him turn noticeably red, and she gave him a winning smile. They immediately proceeded to the Goethe House. Councilor Professor Böffel did the honors. Pschorr made his request. Böffel became suspicious.

"You have brought a mechanical dummy of Goethe's larynx with you. Do I understand you correctly?"

"And I am seeking permission to install it in Goethe's study."

"I see. But to what end? What do you want? What does this mean? The newspapers are full of stories about something strange that happened. No one knows what to make of it. The guards at the vault claim to have seen old Goethe, and he even thundered at one of them. The others were so stupefied by the apparition they had to receive medical attention. The incident was even reported to the Grand Duke."

Anna Pomke gave Pschorr a questioning look. But Abnossah, surprised, asked, "But what has that to do with my request? It certainly is curious—perhaps an actor has allowed himself to make a joke?"

"Ah! You are right, we should investigate that possibility. I couldn't help but ... But how could you have copied Goethe's larynx when you couldn't possibly have modeled it after nature?"

"That's what I would have preferred, but unfortunately I wasn't given permission."

"And I suspect it wouldn't have done you much good, anyway."

"Why is that?"

"To the best of my knowledge, Goethe is dead."

"Please, the skeleton, the skull in particular, would suffice for the precise construction of the model; at least it would be enough for me."

"Your virtuosity is well known, Professor. What do you want with the larynx, if I may ask?"

"I want to reproduce the Goethean organ, as close as possible to its true nature."

"And you have the model?"

"Right here!"

Pschorr quickly opened a case. Böffel let loose an odd scream. Pomke smiled proudly.

"But you could not," cried Böffel, "have modeled this larynx after the skeleton!?"

"I did the next best thing! That is to say, after certain accurate life-size and life-like busts and images. I am very skilled in such things."

"That is well known! But why do you want to put this model in Goethe's old study?"

"He must have said many interesting things there. And the sound waves must still be vibrating there, albeit, of course, exceedingly diminished."

"You believe that?"

"It is not a belief; it is so!"

"Yes?"

"Yes."

"What is it you want to do?"

"I will draw up those vibrations through the larynx."

"What?"

"Exactly as I said!"

"Absurd!—Forgive me, but I can hardly take that seriously."

"All the more reason I insist you give me the opportunity to convince you that I am serious. I don't understand your resistance. I surely can't cause any damage with this harmless apparatus."

"That's not it. I am not resisting, not at all. However, owing to my position I am nevertheless obliged to ask you certain questions. I hope you won't think worse of me for it."

"God forbid!"

There now unfolded in Goethe's study, in the presence of Anna Pomke, Professor Böffels, and a few curious assistants and servants, the following scene.

Pschorr placed his model on a stand in such a way that the mouth, as he referred to it, was installed where the living one would have been situated when Goethe sat. Pschorr then pulled a kind of rubber air bag out of his pocket and sealed off the nose and mouth with one of its open ends. He unfolded the bag and spread it like a blanket out over the top of a small table that he'd pulled over. On this makeshift blanket he placed a most charming miniature phonograph with a microphone mechanism that he took from the small case he had brought with him. He now carefully wrapped the blanket around the phonograph, closed it again in the form of an end with a tiny opening, and screwed into the end opposite the mouth a kind of bellows, which, however, as he explained, was not to blow the air of the room into the opening of the mouth, but rather to draw it out through it.

"If," Pschorr lectured, "I let the model's nasopharynx exhale, as it were, as if while speaking, then this special Goethean larynx functions as a kind of sieve, which only lets through the sound vibrations of the Goethean voice, if there are any; and there are certain to be some. Should they be weak, the machine is equipped with amplification devices."

The whir of the phonograph as it recorded could be heard inside the rubber air bag. A feeling of horror came over them when they thought they could hear the slightest vague whispering inside.

Pomke said, "Oh, please!" and laid her delicate ear against the rubber skin. She started, because inside there was a hoarse rustling:

"As I have said, my dear Eckermann, this Newton was blind with his seeing eyes. How often, my friend, do we see this in someone who appears so open! Therefore, it is the sense of the eye in particular that calls for the criticism of our judgment. Where this is lacking, sense itself is lacking. But the world mocks judgment, it mocks reason. What it earnestly wants is uncritical sensation. I have very often, painfully, experienced this, but I will never tire of contradicting the whole world and, in my way, showing my colors against Newton's."

Pomke heard this with pleased horror. She trembled and said, "Heavenly! Heavenly! Professor, I owe the most beautiful moment of my life to you."

"So, you were able to hear something?"

"Indeed! Quiet, but very clear!"

Pschorr nodded contentedly. He worked the bellows a while more and then said, "That should be enough for now."

He packed all the instruments except the phonograph back into his small case. All those present were eager and shocked. Böffel asked, "Do you truly believe, Professor, that you have captured words once spoken here by Goethe? A genuine echo from Goethe's own mouth?"

"I not only believe it, I am certain of it. I will now have the phonograph play back with the microphone and predict that you will have to agree with me."

The familiar hoarse hissing, throat clearing, and straining. Then, an extraordinary voice rang out, the sound of which electrified everyone present, Abnossah included. They heard the words quoted above. Then it went on: "Well, now! Newton saw it, did he? The continuous color spectrum? But I, my friend, reiterate: he deceived himself—he witnessed an optical illusion and accepted it uncritically, glad to be able to straightaway count, measure, and quibble. The devil take his monism, his continuousness, because it is only the contrast of colors that makes their appearance possible! Oh,

Eckermann! Dear Eckermann! Stay with me! White—
it is neither made of colors, nor does it yield any colors.
Rather it must, through some means, be mechanically
combined with black to make gray; and chemically
united to be able to produce the bright gray of the colors.
And you don't get white by neutralizing color. Rather,
you restore the original contrast of black against white:
of which, of course, you can only see the white in its daz-
zling clarity. I, dear friend, see the darkness just as clear-
ly, and where Newton has only hit white, I, my dearest
friend, have also hit black, dead center. I think that the
lapsed archer in you would greatly admire that! So it is,
and not otherwise! And the distant grand-—and consid-
ering the absurd world, probably even the all-too-distant
great-grand—children, will learn from me to laugh at
Newton!"

Böffel had sat down; everyone was cheering. The
servants stamped their feet in pleasure, like the students
in the fiery lectures of the tremendous revolutionary,
noble Reucken. But Abnossah sternly said, "Gentlemen!
You are interrupting Goethe's speech. He has more to
say!"

There was again silence, and they heard, "No and
again no, my dearest friend! Of course, you could have
done it, if only you had wanted to! It is the will, the will
of these Newtonians that is weak. And a weak will is a
pernicious faculty, an active powerlessness that makes
me shudder, although I see it everywhere, over and over

again, and should be accustomed to it. The will, my good friend, is something you may consider harmless enough, but in truth it is the wellspring of all things great and small, and it is not the divine ability, but rather the will, the divine will, which shames man and shows all his inadequacy. Were you able to desire divinely, the ability would be necessary and not just easy, and, dear friend, much would be everyday experience that now has not even a vague idea that it could venture out without being attacked or ridiculed.

"There was the young Schopenhauer, a youth of supreme promise, full of the most glorious will, but made thoroughly sick by the worm-eating of surfeit, by his own insatiability. Just as, in color theory, the pure sun blinded him so that he credited the night not as another sun, but as a nullity, so the life of this unclouded brilliance so completely captivated him that against its pure radiance human life no longer captivated him in the least; it even seemed reprehensible. Notice, my friend, that the purest, even the most divine will runs the risk of failing, when it asserts itself with absolutely fixity; when it does not grasp wisely and adroitly the conditions, not to mention the limits set by necessity, of its abilities. The will is indeed a magician! It can do anything. But the human will is no will at all: it is an inferior will. Ha! Haha! Hehe! Hi!" Goethe laughed, very mysteriously, then went into a near-whisper: "I can, my valued friend, entrust something to you, reveal something. You will think it a fairy tale, but I have seen it with great clarity. The individual will can overcome fate, can force fate to serve it, provided that it—listen carefully now!—by no means believes that the divinely creative intent and effort which rests and tenses itself within should moreover, in intense deliberateness, be brought forth by way of the most strained musculature. Look at the Earth, how it drives its spinning! What earthly diligence! What ceaselessly moving activity! Now then, Eckermann, this diligence is only earthly, this activity disastrous only in a merely mechanically way—on the other hand, the magical Sun-Will divinely vibrates, resting within itself, and through this highly unusual self-sufficiency develops the electromagnetism that humbles the full host of planets, moons, and comets swarming at its feet in servile submission. Dear friend, to be the one to understand it, to experience in the most completely serene spiritual sense this noble actor!———Enough, more than enough. I have been accustomed to controlling myself when I saw others, often even Schiller, freely rhapsodizing about that divine activity, about which one should only be silent, because all talk would not only be useless and superfluous, but by promoting a foolish common understanding, where it did not promote the most decisive misunderstanding, must become harmful and hindering. Think about it, my trusted friend, and preserve it in your heart without attempting to untangle it! Trust that one day it will untangle itself, and this evening go to the play with little Wölfchen, who is very hungry for it, and because you will be with him, please treat Kotzebue gently, although he disgusts us!"

"My God," Pomke said, as the others eagerly congratulated Abnossah. "My God! I could listen forever! Eckermann withheld so much from us!"

After a long pause the sound of snoring came from the apparatus, then nothing more.

Abnossah said, "Gentlemen, as you can hear, Goethe is asleep. We can expect nothing more for a few hours, if not a full day. Waiting all that while makes no sense. As you can plainly see, the apparatus is aligned so precisely with the reality of the passage of time that at this point we, in the best case, would only hear something more if Eckermann returned to Goethe's after the theater on the same evening. I don't have the time to wait for that."

"How is it," asked Böffel, rather skeptically, "that we were able to listen to this conversation in particular?"

"Coincidence," responded Pschorr. "The conditions, above all the structure of the apparatus and its placement, happened to be such that (as it happened) just these and no other sound vibrations could become active. At best, it was due to my respecting the fact that Goethe was sitting and the placement of his chair."

"Oh, please, please! Abnossah!" (Pomke felt intoxicated, almost in a frenzy; she called him by his first name.) "Try another place! I cannot hear enough—that's true, too, even if's only his snoring!"

Pschorr made the apparatus disappear and buckled the case. He had turned very pale. "My dear Anna—my Lady," he corrected himself, "another time." (His jealousy of dear old Goethe had set his insides churning.)

"How about," Böffel asked, "trying Schiller's skull? That would settle the dispute about whether it is the real one."

"Certainly," said Abnossah, "because if we heard the skull say, 'How about a glass of wine' and it didn't have a Swabian accent, we'd know it wasn't Schiller's skull.— I'm wondering, could the invention be refined? Perhaps I could fabricate a generic larynx that could be adjusted like opera glasses in order to accommodate all sorts of possible vibrations. We could then again hear antiquity and the Middle Ages speak, determine the correct pronunciation of the old idiom. And any esteemed contemporaries who say indecent things aloud could be handed over to the police."

Abnossah offered Pomke his arm, and they went back to the station. They entered the waiting room cautiously, but the locally known woman had already left.

Abnossah said, "What if she handed over her famous brother's larynx to me? But she won't—she will argue that people are not yet mature enough and that the intelligentsia do not have the deep respect of the people, so nothing can be done, my beloved! Beloved! Because (oh!) Such is the case! That is what you are! You!"

But Pomke hadn't heard any of this. She appeared to be daydreaming.

"How he bore down on his *r*s!" she whispered, trembling.

Abnossah snorted angrily. Anna was startled and absentmindedly asked him, "Did you say something, dear Pschorr? I am forgetting the master in favor of his work. But the work dwindles away when I hear Goethe's voice!"

They climbed into the coach for the return journey. Pomke said nothing; Abnossah brooded silently. Once they had passed out of Halle, he threw the case with Goethe's larynx out of the window and under the wheels of a train racing in the opposite direction.

"What have you done?" Pomke cried.

"I have loved," Pschorr sighed, "and soon, also will have lived—and ruined my victorious rival, Goethe's larynx."

Pomke turned a deep red and, laughing, threw herself impetuously into Abnossah's arms, which wrapped tightly around her. At that moment the conductor appeared and requested their tickets.

"Oh, God! 'Nossah," murmured Pomke, "you must, you must make me a new larynx of Goethe, you must—otherwise—"

"There's no 'otherwise'! *Apres les noces*, my dove— after the wedding!"

Prof. Dr. Abnossah Pschorr
Anna Pschorr, b. Pomke
Just married
Presently in Weimar,
At The Elephant

Imagine! Imagine, just this once, an enormous egg, an egg about as big as St. Peter's Basilica, the Cologne Cathedral, and Notre Dame combined. Imagine: I speedily make my way through the desert, and in the middle of the desert (thirst, camel, white bones in yellow-brown sand, a touch of El-se-las-kersch-ül-er, caravan, oasis, jackal, cistern, desert king—pshoo![6]) this magnificent egg rises and curves. Imagine the sun showering down a sparkling light that splashes off the egg. My first thought was Fata (Fairy) Morgana. Can't be! I tap on it. The egg reveals itself under my touch; I feel its temperature. I ask it, "Is anyone in there?" No answer! Anyone else would have passed it by; it would have given them the creeps would be my guess. In such cases, however, I can't rest until I know exactly what's going on. So, I walk around the egg—and right at the height of a man I find a dark green button the size of a walnut. I press it. The egg sinks forcefully into the ground, only the point still peeping out of the desert sand. Imagine how that affected me. But on the top, there was another button the same size. I press it—and a clap like thunder! knocked me back; the egg suddenly but smoothly slid up again. Imagine how I, in the middle of the desert, repeated this game about a hundred times. Just imagine! I was as happy as a child. But eventually, little by little, I grew curious about the deeper meaning of this childish game. So, I examined the egg again, and after an extended effort, I finally found a very faint seam that seemed to extend vertically the entire length of the egg. I look at the push button, touch it, don't push it ... suddenly I turn it—and down it goes! The egg lays itself on its side, the point on which it had stood turned toward me—a most inviting portal, a jasper-yellow egg yolk shines invitingly before me. Imagine how a smile then, as the expression goes, brightens my ugly mug as I read the following inscription on the egg yolk:

> Wanderer in the desert
> who for the first time
> beholds the egg of eggs
> and (imagine!)
> takes childish delight in it,
> know this:
> That this egg alone can
> transform the desert into Eden.
> So!
> Now, free this egg's secret for me!

You, accursed reader, have you forgotten the seam? Now this seam also went vertically over the bulbous egg yolk portal. But there was no button on it. I knock on it, and it sounds like you're pecking your fingertip against your noggin while you're covering your ears. I take another close look at the perfectly circular border between yolk and shell and, just imagine, to the right of the cleft, of the seam, is a more-or-less finger-sized opening; I carefully stick my finger in it. But, imagine this, I can't get it back out. What would you have done then? Found the nearest police station? Ha, better to keep Europe out of this! Besides, no honorable man abandons his finger so lightly. Since I couldn't yank my finger back out, I used my hand to push harder, using all my strength—and, that's right, the yolk on the right rolled itself up. I got my finger free and took a look into the egg. Because I could make out nothing definite, I gave the right half of the yolk a powerful shove upward, and ascended (imagine) into the egg. I felt as if I were walking on yellow snow. Once my eyes had gotten used to the dim half-light, I suddenly saw a wide, beautiful staircase with flat alabaster steps rising before me. Now I climb up to a scenic overlook and marvel at the interior of the egg. The portal is located over here; over there, the apex; below me, yellow snow; above me the desert sun gleams through the joint. Just imagine my situation! At least I discover, overall, nothing more that is strange, except at the apex, where something seemed to lie in wait. There was a stairway on the opposite side of the overlook, and I took it. It led to the apex. And that eternal eggshell curve! The eternal yellow snow, or whatever the stuff was. As I finally stand on the apex, I see at the same moment the portal across the way rolling shut—just imagine. I shout. Here's some good advice I can give you: never shout inside an egg! It creates such a rolling racket that it just adds to your problems.

Not only does the portal roll shut, but I also notice that the egg is rising again. It stands up, the stairs become a steep ladder, with me standing on the top rung. And suddenly, just imagine, I feel the desert-egg speeding deep into the ground again. But for all that, the pleasant twilight continued, because, you see, the eggshell was phosphorescing. And now, finally, the strangest thing of all happened: the egg spoke to me. That is, it phosphoresced to me so articulately that I instinctively understood it. Just imagine, the egg claimed that the recovery of the entire desert hinged on its destruction. A wisecracking egg! (I smiled quite a big smile.) The egg then lit up to me with the well-known proposition: "The desert is growing."[7]

And had I not noticed that the egg could rise and sink? Well, yes, I had! It now told me I should climb down the ladder to the portal below, open it, and clear away a small but offensive hindrance down there. I would then hear (or rather, see) more. Meanwhile, my only thought was: How do I get out of this creepy egg, and quickly? But, on the contrary, on top of everything else, I had to slip into the oblivion under the egg! But the egg phosphoresced kindly to me, so I could climb down with confidence, and as if on gentle wings I felt myself carried more than climbing down. The portal, however, did not allow itself to be opened as easily. Imagine this, too: I was several hundred meters below the surface of the Earth, and I had no way of knowing what hell would break loose if I rolled the egg yolk down there up again. When I hesitated, I was phosphorescently encouraged again. I finally found the small opening with my finger and pushed the thing up. The opening had barely yawned when a storm rushed out of it, and in a quick moment, so fast that I lost my breath, I was thrown up against the tip of the egg, and before I knew what was happening, the tip flipped back, flipped outward, like a lid, and I was lying in the desert sand.

Escape! was my first thought—a kingdom for a camel, or a dromedary! No such desert ship anywhere in sight. Instead—just imagine—how amazed I was when I discovered that someone had crawled out of the egg behind me, a sort of mummy with bandages and wrappings. The lady (or do you think it was a gentleman?) told me the following, in a language that, strangely enough, though I had never heard it before I immediately understood (imagine it as being a music without a scale):

"Meddlesome, foolish, fearful, but not unsympathetic fellow! Chance, harmless worldling, has honored you! Now that, making your ridiculous pilgrimage through the sick mystery of my desert, you are touched by my breath, you are no longer insignificant enough to misunderstand my intentions. Understand, the desert is the same as what the Earth is, only more so, *leonum arida nutrix,* almost barren, because you wrenched the principle of fertility out of the center of its sphere, left it lying withered and peeled on the surface, and I, the soul of souls, became a mummy, and only because of you, exalted fool, I have been electrified. You are now overtaken by your own deed! Finish it! When I am again inside the egg and the tip snaps shut, push the button. To the same extent that the egg sinks slowly, slowly but unerringly safely to the Earth's center, it becomes smaller and smaller, but more concentrated in its fertile power, and when it arrives at the center, is completely crushed and compressed, radiant through and through, it releases it, outward, upward, into all the heavens. You, my good man, little louse of insignificance, will feel it, too: living means being gifted with genius, feeling divine and acting like it. Well now!"

Do you perchance know the genteel old baron who on similar occasions says, "Madness, madness!" a hundred times straight?[8] I let the mummy hop calmly over the eggshell edge. I admit I also calmly closed the lid of the egg again. But the button? I never touched it again! I reached back, seized my coattails, floured yellow with egg dust as they were, and tucking them under my arms, I ran away from there faster than any camel could have.

What does "principle of fertility" really mean here? Should I overpopulate the Earth? Should I (of all people) allow an old mummy to get me into trouble? God knows, the Earth is not a bowl of custard, least of all one *aux confitures*.[9] Should the salvation of the world depend on a trifle? On pressing a button? After all, I no longer know where the egg is to be found. But if the reader would so desire, then this egg would be highly recommended as the object of your next Easter egg hunt. Because even though I ran away like a coward—who knows! Perhaps it takes greater courage to grasp a near and tremendous happiness than to merely suspect an adventurous distant one, while overcoming tremendous dangers. We should cross-examine ourselves! Consider: would you now, immediately, on the spot, with a light push of your finger, want to bring about happiness for the masses, the salvation of the entire world? Wouldn't you be more terrified of that than of any of your more comfortable martyrdoms??——

And yet, in my deepest thoughts, I secretly shed a good many tears over that egg of the desert: I should have—oh, yes!—I really should have pressed it—!

———

—said Clara. And just as her expression was about to dissolve, I composed myself, got ahead of her, and let mine dissolve before hers.

"But what did your dad say?"

"Oh, in the end my dad can just—"

"For God's sake!"

"—not hold me back."

That's how our love began.

(*To be continued*)

(*Continuation*)

Peace broke out, as sudden as a thunderstorm. The tree-tops of the townspeople shriveled. The children lost the sweet illiteracy from their (as Auntie said) tiny faces. Peace settled on the street where our little house stands, and it soon looked like the Tower of Pisa, you know, the toilet with its center of gravity almost falling past the fulcrum point of the house chapel. Miessauer's love song to Albania rang out at the gates.[10] Then Clara said to me:

"The country at peace! Breathe a sigh of relief, you doves rumbling above the London of my no longer stormy bosom."[11]

I laughed as only the happily at peace can laugh—to wit:

> *. . . that more lightly bite the fleas,*
> *who shortly before were hopping on you,*
> *and the lice that pinched*
> *freshly plucked from your skin.*

(To be continued)

(Continuation)
Clara had now finally become an old woman, who hardly remembered me. I myself have been resting from my wanderings a long while (in the graveyard of suicides). Our young generation was already celebrating their fiftieth birthdays. Her clothes had pockets where she could clench her fists. Otherwise, everything was so amiable; even death smiled mischievously, and lovely dimples showed in his cheeks. Then—a Wednesday, I think—I came careening out of my tomb. A long veil of desperation fluttered gauzily over the buried ones; out of our graves we rolled like flower-bedecked floats in the festival parade. We rushed to the city. I stopped my casket car

in front of the house of my elderly widow. "What do you think of me now? Do you want to laugh or cry?"

(To be continued)

✳

(Continuation)

My tomb companions had by now also stopped here and there. And their "loved ones," who like to call themselves "ours," came out. They came over, they hurried, they were embarrassed. Clara came, too:

"How have you arranged your shroud so, Helmut-Hinrich? Still as theatrical as ever—as at your height, as—" a trickle of tears emerged from beneath her delicate, withered lids, and the sun. I mean, the sun shone as warm as gold around the old form, so unspeakably ironic, so different. There are stirrings, very faint, imperceptible, until you die the death of the dead. I had created some children with Clara; they looked out the windows, they waved their handkerchiefs. I rattled up with bony fingers like castanets and hammered my skull on the underside of the cover. But:

"Adieu now, my dear ones,
"We must part!"[12]

(To be continued)

✳

(*Continuation*)

Clara wanted to come with me; I advised her against it. Leave your other foot, I pleaded, don't you know that you already have one where I am now jumping with both. Another kiss. Then another. Then two. Another $\sqrt[\infty]{\infty}$°°°°°°°°°°°°°°° kisses. A look of refractive-power $\left(\frac{4^\infty}{5} \cdot \frac{8}{1000}\right)^\infty$—and

"Go now, go now ..." oh, "quick, quick, quick!" much less so. No, all the trumpets of Jericho are our horns. "The casket cars," it said in a report, "just passed through our locality. The head authorities had lined up, with youngsters from the school, to welcome them. Mayor Verbogen gave the keynote speech, in which he convincingly proved that it was only and exclusively the suicides who developed a very special talent for immortality. A telegram of homage was sent to His Excellency Häckel."

(*To be continued*)

(*Continuation*)

Scarcely had we, with just a few movements, converted our casket cars into casket airships when Fritz M . . . . r, up in the glorious clean heaven, offered to let us hold talks with them. He showed us samples—not bad at all! However, the usefulness of heaven for discretion from our loved ones should not be impaired. We told him we didn't give a damn about that but were reluctant to talk to them. It was terribly difficult for this old mouthpiece to understand that he was completely superfluous. He had inadvertently come near the point opposite H. von Kleist's mouth, and von Kleist gathered an Aeolus out of one of his Anecdotes and let it noisily fly.

(*To be continued*)

(*Continuation and Conclusion*)
But it is the broken off that triumphs. If you should ever get to heaven by our unusual route, let go of every consequence. Not in those, never in those, your heaven rests and revels only in what you have broken off. You sigh. Interrupt your sighing. Interrupt the thoughts and moods that consequently want to attach themselves to it! Eat a peach, put its pit in your (already waiting) appendix. Never forget that you are only gathered here for entertainment! The "forget-me-not" is the worst of flowers, because it was only because of it that the grave on which it blooms was invented.—

TISSUE! TISSUE!

A man went walking. He had a barometer on the front of his jacket and a thermometer on the back. He was annoyed that all the weather houses were stationary. He wanted to be a living, walking weather house.

The man walked up to people and popped the cover of his watch under their noses: "Do you want to know," he said warmly, "what time it is? Please!"—People didn't like it. They considered it a nuisance; they got impatient. But Boboll (that was the man's name) drew their attention to his thermometer. At this, they gave him an annoyed look and walked away. But he didn't allow this, he hastily ran ahead of them and prevented them from going on. Turning around he said, "Back here you can also check the barometer reading."

At that, people surrounded him; they never let him go. They looked at him with affection and he walked contentedly in their midst. From his pockets he drew packets of perfumed tissue and happily handed them out. He gave the ladies safety pins and powdering paper. A rich gentleman who had taken something offered him money—but he refused, and asked in all innocence, "Am I a vending machine? I do this voluntarily." Then the rich gentleman blushed with joy, and everyone cheered and rejoiced along with him. Many shouted "Sixty-eight degrees in the shade!" Some showed others the fine paper, and someone said, "I think his back barometer is going down." At this, the younger members of the crowd howled so incessantly that the entire troop, with Boboll in the center, was surrounded by policemen and asked to disperse. They wanted to arrest Boboll because they thought he was a street vendor without a license. But the rich gentleman cleared up this misunderstanding. And as the policemen heard and saw the details, they grew cheerful and felt in good spirits. They all said in one voice, "Looney," and tapped their forefingers against their powerful foreheads.

At the station Boboll announced that he was a philanthropist, and with his modest means he unfortunately could only do so much. However, he has a sure eye for the small needs of passersby. Certain needs must, however, first be awakened. Nearly everyone feels the need for some small comfort. Boboll took a velvet brush out of his pocket, a three-part hand mirror, a tilting writing desk, a telescope, and other useful things.

The policemen watched Boboll for a long while, but he maintained his simple demeanor and pleasant expression. The policemen finally advised him not to help passersby—indeed, they forbade him from doing so—because it was a nuisance, because it created crowds. They gave him a stern warning and they let it be known he would be arrested for the next incident. Then they released him and it was a long while before they could get over him.———

Boboll walked through the passersby and again clearly felt their needs. He took a top hat from a gentleman. It was a rosy, excited youth who was all in a rush. But Boboll took out his small brush, and as he smoothed the silk hat, he did not answer the young man's excited questions, but presented him the shining adornment. The lad first struck Boboll's ear with the hat, then put it on his head and quickly started to move along. But Boboll asked him if he needed tissue and said if he wanted to know the barometer reading to look in back; the thermometer was in front. And Boboll let him look into the three-part mirror, as well. The elegant but crude fellow struck him, then pushed him down onto a heap so that he lay in manure. The mirror tinkled into pieces, and a piece of tissue flew violently from a distance into Boboll's right eye. Unsuspecting, sympathetic passersby helped Boboll get back on his feet. They freed him from the shards of the mirror and the other glass instruments. But Boboll, still shaken, was already scanning their faces. Oh! There was so much that he could guess with precision: almost everyone needed paper, pins, time- and other pieces. Some had forgotten the date; or they wanted to quickly jot something down; or they had an itch they couldn't reach. A woman had been crying and needed powder; one gentleman was missing a button in an awkward place. These were trifling needs—certainly! But Boboll found his happiness in satisfying them, even though he was aware he was no longer allowed to do so.

This loss was no trifling matter to him, it rendered him useless, it was the end, it was death. Boboll could only function one way, only as this small god of passers-by, or not at all. Resolved to give up his life along with his helping of others, he only thought about how he could at least bring a little joy to passersby through his death. He donated his fortune to the establishment of a Mobile Institute of Satisfaction: here people could find all the little things they were missing, things Boboll was no longer allowed to give them himself. Boboll thought it would be very apt to have his corpse cremated and the urn with his ashes placed on that wagon, to ride there forever. But he suddenly had a much happier idea.

Have you noticed how many gentlemen there are who lament the loss of a close friend until they finally discover his body in the morgue? Well, then! Boboll wanted to let himself die. He studied public notices, police reports, and kiosks, and finally managed to find an appropriate dead man who had been reported missing, someone who, by all indications, must have roughly resembled him. A search was on for the body of Edgar Schiebedonkel, a hospital worker, which had probably been sold to an anatomical institute by a guard. Boboll got hold of a photograph of Schiebedonkel and carefully made himself up to match it—gave himself a rummy's nose, a bald head, a scar, and several gaps between his teeth. Boboll even laid out big money for some of Schiebedonkel's old underwear and clothes. But as soon as he vividly imagined the heartfelt joy of the family and of the exonerated guard when Schiebedonkel's corpse was finally found in the morgue, no sacrifice seemed too small a detail to become the direct source of such delight.

His will concluded with this passage: "In order not to deprive the foundation which I hereby establish of even a single penny, I am stuffing dynamite charges into my head and everywhere in my body they will go. I am going to burst and leave no remains, and so save the cost of a funeral, to the benefit of all passersby."———

So it came to pass that one fine day the guard and the Schiebedonkel family unhesitatingly identified the dead Edgar in the morgue. Had you been there you could have really seen something: Edgar's corpse was smiling! They would not have thought it possible, but they saw it! True goodness, genuine philanthropy gives even your corpse a jovial appearance.

And as the Schiebedonkel family and the guard were bringing the dead Boboll, whom they had taken for Edgar (the guard surprised and happy), to his grave, the hearse collided with the wreathed front end of the Mobile Institute of Satisfaction, on whose platform an old man was shouting, "Tissue!"———

Fear not, gentle reader! We want to talk about something else. Please come to the Street of Zeppelins. Right! We are already there. Do you see a balloon hangar? Right! We are going inside, we are going to make an ascent, fly over every country on Earth inside an hour—while remaining in this balloon hangar.

As you know, you already can travel in a similar way over water and land, under the illusion that you are seated on a moving ship or in a railroad car, with painted scenery rolling by outside the windows. The aeronautics airship journey that we are now planning will delight you through the thoroughness of its illusion. In this theater, built specifically to exactly reproduce the experience of air travel, the auditorium is suspended high above the screen of the stage. You are familiar with the technique known as the haunted swing: where the viewer sits is stable, while the room around him is movable, so that the ceiling and floor can become confused with one another, and the viewer becomes disoriented and dizzy. All rooms meant for presentations should be set up following this example: the popular horizontal movie theater, in which the screen is in front of the viewer, could then easily be transformed in such a way that the viewer would first see himself as being below, now as above, the screen. This could produce the most dazzling displays.

Here it is as if we were entering the gondola gallery of a giant airship. These gondola galleries are attached to the ceiling of a hall, and this ceiling is modeled on the underside of a balloon. From this balloon vault, the parallel ring system of four galleries hangs down on ropes and cords. Seats are attached in such a way that the audience can look down over both balustrades. The innermost gallery has only one balustrade, on the outer side. Its circular space is completed on the inside by a floor. Under this floor is the technician's booth and the projection apparatus, whose photographs were taken on the occasion of real airship flights. Incidentally, the sound of the apparatus is like the roar of the propeller of an airship and so serves to reinforce the illusion.

In perpendicular depths under these galleries, the stage lies as if in an abyss. If you took a sleeper to one of these galleries and woke him there, and he then saw the rigging and the balloon above him, heard the roar as from a propeller, and looked into the depths, he would be convinced that London was passing by below—he would never suspect it was an illusion. Descent and ascent can be reproduced with the greatest of ease: the reel of film used for the ascent is run in reverse. The first image immediately throws you inescapably into the illusion. You hover over the hall of this same theater in which you are sitting; you go upward, and you see, from a bird's eye view, the wider and wider surroundings. The pace is picking up, and a series of increasingly distant landscapes and cities are moving by before your eyes. You fly over mountains, seas, streams; beneath you the entire Earth rolls past.

But this is nothing compared to the tremendous intensification of the illusion when the apparatus ultimately projects astronomical bodies, and you can truly believe you have been transported among the stars. These images are artificial, but very ingenious. Their sequence begins with rising from the globe; you see, for example, the sea with a few islands below you; it sinks into the depths and suddenly, magically, becomes spherical. The curvature grows smaller and smaller—suddenly it lies far below you as a globe, and you are in space without solid ground, until you approach a new celestial body, such as the moon, Mars, very far from the sun.

How? You say there's no Street of Zeppelins, nor any such movie theater? You are wrong! Cinema entrepreneurs are far from being so stupid as to neglect creating such a setup. And, incidentally, you should instead suspect that the entire world is already just such a vertical industry—and not just optically, but convincingly for all the senses. *Adieu*!———

NOTES

1. A variation on the first two lines of Schiller's riddle, "*Wir stammen, unser sechs Geschwister*," which Goethe used as a motto in his book *Zur Farbenlehre* [Theory of Colors]. This refers to the six color sectors Goethe proposed as part of this theory.

2. A reference to Berthold Schwarz, a fourteenth-century German alchemist who was believed by some to be the inventor of gunpowder.

3. A "miracle of meaning by chance" is from Nietzsche: "Wunder von Sinn im Zufall," in *Ecce homo*.

4. Adapted from Nietzsche, *Beyond Good and Evil.*

5. Max Scheler (1874–1928) was a German philosopher who supported German militarism during World War I. His *Der Genius des Kriegs und der Deutsche Krieg* [The genius of war and the German war] was published in 1915. The woman Mynona is mocking here is Elisabeth Foerster-Nietzsche, Friedrich Nietzsche's younger sister. She edited his

unpublished writings to suit her own ideas; she was later supported financially by the National Socialists.

6. Else Lasker Schüler (1869–1945) was a poet and playwright, one of the few women writers associated with the expressionist movement.

7. From Nietzsche's *Zarathustra* ["*Die Wüste wächst!*"], an image of the growth of nihilism.

8. Possibly a reference to the fabulous Baron von Munchausen.

9. "With jam."

10. A deliberate satirical misrepresentation: "love" for "hate," "Albania" for "Albion." Ernst Lissauer (1882–1937) was a German poet and dramatist, most famous for his poem *Haßgesang gegen England* [Song of hate for England].

11. "Rumpler Taube," literally "rumbling dove," was the name of a single-engine German bomber from the World War I era.

12. From Justinus Kerner's *Wanderlied* (1809). This poem, and others by Kerner, was set to music by Robert Schumann in 1840, in his Opus 35, 12 *Gedichte von Justinus Kerner*.

W. C. Bamberger has translated works by Paul Scheerbart, Oscar A. H. Schmitz, and Bess Brenck Kalischer, among others. His published essays have addressed subjects ranging from the language of poet Anne Carson to the death of Kierkegaard to Guy Davenport's "friendly trees." His ebook *The Reflective Head*, on Michael Ayrton's large 1972 sculpture, is available from *Raft Magazine*. He lives in Michigan.

OTHER GERMAN AUTHORS PUBLISHED BY WAKEFIELD PRESS

Hugo Ball
   Flametti, or The Dandyism of the Poor

Otto Julius Bierbaum
   Samalio Pardulus

Curt Corrinth
   Potsdamer Platz, or The Nights of the New Messiah: Ecstatic Visions

Bess Brenck Kalischer
   The Mill: A Cosmos

Erich Mühsam
   *Psychology of the Rich Aunt: Being an Inquiry, in Twenty-Five
   Parts, into the Question of Immortality*

Mynona
   The Creator
   My Papa and the Maid of Orléans and Other Grotesques
   The Unruly Bridal Bed and Other Grotesques

Oskar Panizza
   The Pig, in Poetic, Mythological, and Moral-Historical Perspective

Paul Scheerbart
  Lesabéndio: An Asteroid Novel
  Munchausen and Clarissa: A Berlin Novel
  The Perpetual Motion Machine: The Story of an Invention
  Rakkóx the Billionaire & The Great Race
  The Stairway to the Sun & Dance of the Comets

Oscar A. H. Schmitz
  Hashish

Walter Serner
  At the Blue Monkey: 33 Outlandish Stories

Unica Zürn
  The Trumpets of Jericho